Because It's Here

Because It's Here

Jane Merchant

ABINGDON PRESS

Nashville  New York

Acknowledgments

My thanks to the editors of the following publications in which many of these poems previously appeared:

Arizona Highways, Author and Journalist, Bible Teacher for Adults, Capper's Farmer, Capper's Weekly, Chatelaine, The Christian Family, Christian Herald, The Christian Home, Christian Science Monitor, The Church School, Classmate, Country Gentleman, Epworth Notes, Farm Journal, Good Housekeeping, Kaleidograph, Kansas City Star and *Times, Ladies' Home Journal, Life and Health, The Lyric, McCall's, Mature Years, The New York Herald-Tribune, The New York Times, Open Windows,* The Poetry Society of Tennessee *Yearbook, The Progressive*

Farmer, Radio Mirror, Saturday Evening Post, Successful Farming, Sunday Nighter, These Times, This Day, Together, Upward, Wall Street Journal, The War Cry, Wesley Quarterly, and *The Youth's Instructor.*

Preface

The title *Because It's Here* suggested to one friend the saying of our frugal forebears, "Eat it up, wear it out, make it do."

That is not exactly what I had in mind in choosing the title, but it is fairly near. In most of these poems my attention is focused on the small delights (and exasperations) of life on this irreplaceable earth rather than on the remote possibilities of life on other planets. Our own small earth is here for us to treasure and tend. I surely do not advocate for earth the fearfully prevalent policy of "Eat it up, wear it out"—and go on to some other planet. My desire, rather, is "make it do." All the resources for joyous human life for all people are here, if we will conserve and use them wisely instead of wasting them. Even when one's personal situation here is discouraging—and whose is not at times?—we can still "make it do" well with the help of patience and humor; and, I hope, with some help from these poems.

This book is dedicated to my friend Eva Venable, because her friendship is always, in sorrow and joy, sustainingly here.

Jane Merchant

Contents

Because It's Here

Because It's Here

Men travel to the moon because it's there
And dance upon its dust because they can—
And in forbidding bleakness note how fair
The little flowering habitat of man.
Yet many of us need not go beyond
One tiny tended garden spot to gaze
At earth with grateful wonder and respond
With interest to its creatures' varied ways.
We honor valiant astronauts who test
Man's skill and knowledge in fantastic flight
Yet follow any redbird's course with zest
And feel immediate intimate delight
When minor galaxies of blooms appear
On earth we cherish well because it's here.

Fabulous

The man in the moon, the knowing oldsters say,
Was shut in there for gathering sticks on Sunday.
Oh, may there be no penalties, we pray,
For Armstrong and for Aldrin now that they
Have gathered rocks upon the moon on Sunday!

View from Earth

Since conscientious astronauts have told
The nitty-gritty truth about the moon's
Dull granulated surface, will its gold
Aspect be one of our unvalued boons?
When Luna, changeling orb of mystery,
Is base for automated laboratories
For cosmic data, will it cease to be
Acknowledged sovereign of our harvest glories?
Of course it will not. Any lightest fluff
Of new moon in a peachbloom evening sky,
Or full moon gilding clouds, has power enough
To capture any earthling's heart and eye
And to dispel with immemorial glow
All drab unlikely facts our minds may know.

First Blush of Spring

Air warms and softens, and skies of evening hint
At pink, and the dove's breast bears a deepening blush
Gently repeated in the roseate tint
Touching the pussy willow's silvery plush.

In Garden Air

Two white butterflies
Dance where, last winter, I saw
Two snowflakes vanish.

Home-grown

No evidence that others bring
Of punctualities of spring,
No shower of jasmine gold, no hoard
Of jonquil treasures, can afford
Such confident delight to me
As comes when I at last can see
On my own soil the valiant blue
Of tiny scillas peeping through.
Only when blossomings appear
On earth of mine can spring be here.

Smoke of Spring

Burn out the last of winter;
Transform to wings of smoke
All wrinkled leaves remaining,
All branches wild winds broke.

New leaves are coming, coming;
Give to the rising wing
The debris of last winter,
The glory of last spring.

Renewal

For all that lives in this green world today
I thank Thee, Lord of life; for every spear
Of vital grass responding to each ray
Of sun; each bloom spontaneously here
In vivid actuality; each wren,
Sparrow and starling, jay and mockingbird
That celebrates renewal of life again
As if no other spring had ever occurred.
And most I thank Thee for life spared to one
So much akin to the essential urge
That pushes grasses upward toward the sun
And causes buried blossoms to emerge
The grave could win no triumph—for one who
Walks youthful earth again at eighty-two.

Who Works with Earth

Who works with soil and sunshine,
Who works with rain and seed,
Shall find rich satisfaction
Of many an urgent need.

Who works with earth and weather
To him shall be revealed
Abiding treasure hidden
In each resurgent field.

Growing Green

Turn out your eyes to pasture.
Look at the growing green
Of grass on yonder valleys
And on the hills between.

Why dull your sight with staring
At words while meanings pass?
One will be much the wiser
Whose mind has gone to grass.

Out of Fashion

Who will praise the snowy laces
Lightly frilling all the air?
Who exult in chilly graces
Budding trees and bushes wear?

Furbelows we welcomed gladly
With the winter just begun
Ruffle many tempers sadly
When we thought the winter done!

Spring Blizzard

Her heart had not consented
That leaf should come, nor bloom,
To that steep hill, tormented
By one new tiny tomb.

Why should one green leaf flourish?
Why should one blossom flower
Or earth have buds to nourish?
Hers closed within an hour.

When grass and petaled branches
Were buried under wild
White whirling avalanches
She sat alone and smiled.

Again the Dogwoods

Again the dogwoods lift white ranks of crosses,
Memorials to battalions of the slain,
Memorials to our spirits' myriad losses,
The white transfigurations of our pain.

Natural Reaction

Now there are doubtless many who would say
With hearty self-assurance that I should
Confront this dull rheumatic-looking day
As if it were the ultimate of good,
But since I can't be always altogether
Blithesome and joyous I prefer to be
Sad on a day of dreary doleful weather
Rather than on one meant for gaiety.
When nature plans a day for gloom I use it
Feeling it most unnatural to refuse it.

Wind

I don't know why the wind's complaining so,
Whining around the rafters half the day
As if it had a toothache in its toe,
As if it had the national debt to pay.

It could be in the treetops cutting capers,
It could be turning cloudlets inside out.
Instead it moans as if it read the papers—
The wind has had some bitter blow, no doubt.

Apple Tree

This is the tree that every child climbs first.
This is the tree we can't remember learning,
The tree we always knew. Its name is a burst
Of juicy tartness in our mouths, returning
To us the tang of earliest delight.
Its name is April and a lyric foam
Of delicately wistful pink and white.
Its name is another synonym for home—
And yet a synonym for places where
We never were at home except in dream;
The gardens of Hesperides, the fair
And unknown isles where golden apples gleam;
Tree of familiar noons and fabled dawns,
Of vanished Edens and suburban lawns.

Remedies

When wounds in the being are raw and new
Lay a web daintily cool with dew
Over them, or a delicate mist
Of snowflakes caught in an amethyst
Tulip chalice, or bind the gauze
Of a rainbow over the mark of claws.
By noon and dawning take scrupulous heed
To gather simples for mortal need.

Not Totally Silent

There are at least
Two robins vigilantly seizing
Worms belonging, presumably, to me,
Building customary nests
In the traditional apple tree,
And flinging airy compliments to heaven
When not entirely preoccupied with food.

These robins have not heard of DDT.

I have not poisoned earthworms or the earth
Yet I cannot be certain, as I would,
The lunch jubilantly extracted, alert eyes
    seeing that it is good,
Will nourish song.

Robins in apple trees have been the subjects
Of much embarrassing verse;
But if a child should say, "What is a robin?"—
What ghastly prose.

I do not wish to be the sole possessor
Of my earth's worms.

And So the Tree

The verdict given—"We will plant another,"
We said, "another dogwood tree, to bear
White blossoms every spring. And if no other
Can be as dear as this one, doubly fair
For long companionship in pure delight,
Let us not mar its beauty with our sadness.
Remember it all glorious in white,
Remember it with gratitude, with gladness."
And so the tree, our tall proud joy, is gone,
Each springtime's best delight for fifteen years,
And its young substitute is growing on.
Slowly the empty area disappears
And bounteous blossoms stir us to renewed
Emotions of gladness and of gratitude.

Trillium

Spring's dainty white
Three-petaled signature of all delight
Must surely be
Named for a fledgling bird's first melody.

Color Transparency

I hold a square of cardboard to the light
(Inches are its dimensions, two by two)
And see inset, jewel perfect and jewel bright,
The glow of April green and April blue
In earth and sky, and vivid hues of phlox,
Forget-me-nots, and pansies blooming gaily
In every smallest crevice of the rocks
Around a pool that birds delight in daily.
This shining view, projected on a screen,
Enlarged, could hardly give a larger measure
Of wondering delight in blue and green
And flower tints, than the keen marveling pleasure
Of seeing perfectly before one's eyes
April in little, April fairy size.

Rain and a Cardinal

Again and again the redbird came.
I left my work, unheeding,
To watch him weaving ribbons of flame
Through silver beading.

Word to the Wind

From the city maple
With lopped-off limbs
A small winged seedlet
Flutters and skims
Free on the gay wind—
Blow, wind, blow!
Carry it far
As a wind can go
Away from the city,
That it may be
In a great green meadow
A great green tree.

Impulsive

Oh, ever as the city springtimes pass
My country heart grows more inclined to yield
All of the city's careful plots of grass
For one large unpremeditated field!

Feast

A prevalence of wings today,
Bright gusto in the garden
As cardinals flaunt in red array
And towhee, mockingbird, and jay
Flash to and fro, excited, gay,
And ask nobody's pardon.

They came for cornbread offerings—
We really couldn't spare it
But know they relish choicest things
And homemade cornbread always brings
A jubilance of lifting wings
To hearts of those who share it.

Dandified

Upon my puzzled
Vision flashes
Sparrows sporting
Gray moustaches.

"It's dandelions,"
My friend explains.
"They eat the seeds—
The fluff remains."

Rediscovered

The scent of iris bloom surprises me
Again this spring; the delicate unintrusive
Fragrance that merely seems about to be
Rather than being; ethereal, elusive.
Perfumes of roses, lilacs, violets
My heart recalls with glad anticipation
In winter, but invariably forgets
This exquisitely subtle emanation.
What good refreshment every year to find
What memory cannot keep through winter hours;
That iris, most meticulously designed,
Most intricately perfect of all flowers,
Should have, for all its regal grace of blooming,
An aura evanescent, unassuming.

Spring Pine

Our year-round Christmas tree now lifts
Slim golden tapers of all sizes
Above red roses' festive gifts
And peonies' colorful surprises.

Days of Grace

In a fair new grace of green
Tranquilly the maples sway
Nodding, pleasantly serene,
To the courteous winds of May.

This politeness may be brief—
Disrespectful winds may blow
Every freshly dainty leaf
Rudely, gustily to and fro,

Causing an indignant flurry
Of immaculate attire,
Angry flouncings, and a hurry
None could possibly admire.

But today trees nod and wave
Innocent of any fright,
And the decorous winds behave
As if they were born polite.

Good Morning

A morning sky of rose and blue,
A lawn all luminous with dew,
And—"Oh," exulted little May,
"Oh, what a pretty little day!"

For Us

Keep this softly shimmering day
In your memory, and if ever
I forget, repeat the way
The air was soft as if it never
Once had been too hot or cold,
Wet or dry, or ever would,
And remind me how the sky
Was blue so deeply, purely good
It seemed that all its centuries past
Of being gently luminous
Were practice so that it, at last,
Could be this perfect blue for us.
Memorize it all, and let
Me never be far away from you
Lest I ever should forget
Or doubt this perfect day was true.

Sky for Realists

Spreading blue over the valleys
In vivid, abundant supply
Bluebonnets give practical people
A down-to-earth sky.

Message

I won't be there
In the bobolink meadows
Where daisies stare
Unblinking, at sun.

If you can wander
In meadowlark pastures,
The singing yonder
That cities deny,

Oh, send me a white ray
Plucked from a daisy,
One small warm light ray
Confirming love.

Surprise

Showers fall from sunny skies, and housewives snatch
Clean clothes from lines, and people trying to catch
A bus, deplore clouds' eccentricity.

Showers fall from sunny skies, and a mocker clings
Among crab apple blossoms, shaking his wings,
Bathed in exuberant felicity.

Field

In this harmonious
Community of green
A solitary blade
Of grass is seldom seen
By placid looker-on
Or languid passerby.
Anonymous multitudes
Content the casual eye.

But, plucked for expert blowing
By some discerning boy,
The individual blade
Whistles specific joy.

Bee Balm

The shredded purple of bee balm under the window
Has been discovered by a prosperous bee
So handsomely arrayed in golden fashion
I wonder a little, what need of balm has he?

Were his deep buzzings derided or misquoted?
Did a thorn prick him as a word pricked me?
Summer has honey for insistent bumblers—
So I am comforted, to some degree.

Theatrical

Cardinals come
Day after day
Brushing the dullness
Of life away
With a casual lift
Of a red, red feather—
Red so incredible
Altogether
That I greet its wearers
Each time, with a brief
Glad suspension
Of unbelief.

For Brightness

Since joy comes seldom now, since sun caressing
The earthbound stars of lemon lilies brings
Solace and peace and a gentle glow of blessing
But never exulting joyfulness that sings—
I am more grateful now for lilies swaying
In golden opulence without alloy
Than ever, needing comfort in dismaying
Events more than I ever needed joy.

For Early Eyes

Our dogwood's white hosannas
Made springtime luminous.
Its crimson hallelujahs
In fall brought joy to us;

But not until this summer
Did there come shining through
Its lifted singing greenness
Pure psalmodies of blue.

Boughs garlanded with blossoms
For early eyes to see
Have made our favorite dogwood
A morning-glory tree!

Rarer Than Star Dust

So exquisitely accurate
The flight of dragonflies,
Their swift pursuits so delicate,
Ethereal, precise,
One has more chance of being hit
By a meteor than by one
Of them—yet one this moment lit
Beside me in the sun!

Michigan to Tennessee

"Those marvelous red banks along the roads
With green vines growing over them!" she said.
"They're like green velvet on the shaded sides
And where the light falls green lace over red.
I never saw the like of them before
And I have traveled on two continents.
Your Tennessee is lovely, but those are
The most enchanting sights the state presents."
"I've always loved," I said, "red banks along
The usual roads I've traveled all my days
But I supposed my love a native thing.
How glad I am at learning from your praise
That those who know a richly different loam
Admire, as well as I, the banks of home."

Capture

The silver-gray cloud-spiders,
Spinning a subtle skein,
Have delicately snared the world
In shimmering webs of rain.

Smoky Haze

The haze upon these Smoky Mountains (so
The Cherokees have told it, they who know)
Is from peace councils that went on and on
With hard words said before the smoke was gone
From the pipe of peace, again and yet again,
Till the Great Spirit turned the quarreling men
To Indian pipes with downcast heads, and spoke
His just decree that airy mists of smoke
Shall lie upon the mountains in all weather
Till all men learn to live in peace together.

How good if all peace conferences that wear
Away in bitterness could fill the air
With so much beauty! We who love this haze
Upon our mountains long for peaceful days;
But till all wars and discords finally cease
There is no lovelier substitute for peace.

At Newfound Gap, the Smokies

Here we look down on mountains; here we gaze
Earthward at peaks mysterious in haze
And valleys so deep our plunging eyes might fall
Bruised in the depths of them except that all
Are soft with mist. We do not speak aloud.
We who look down on mountains are not proud.

On Lonesome Mountains

In cabins built of cumbrous logs
On lonesome mountains in the sky
My forebears lived and loved and hated,
And haunt me always till I die.

Coloring homespun with pokeweed berries,
Weaving a lightsome coverlid—
How can a body so well remember
Doing the things she never did?

I never sighed to a dulcimer
Yet homesick am I for the sound,
And when lost winds blow down the valley
The yearnings of a lonesome hound,

I mind how warmly the backlog burned
As the spinning wheel of an evening whirled;
But that was all in another day
In another life, in another world.

Mule Barn

The new mule barn was once a country church
The congregation, prospering, sold for lumber
And built a fine one. Now the red mules lurch
And sway from side to side in rhythmic slumber
In stalls constructed of converted pews
With all the drowsy rectitude of deacons
Who half awaken, now and then, to muse
On places where the pastor's sermon weakens.
A portly pigeon occupies the rafter
Exhorting with admonitory mien
And mules emerge immediately after
He ends with faces unctuously serene
To testify that they have seen the light—
Though still inclined at times to kick and bite.

Garden in Drought

Dry parchment earth
Is scribbled with wavering lines; faint elegies
For little withered plants.

Taste for Song

The wild black cherries hang high and too far out
Upon the limbs for easy human picking,
Though one may, if he has the heart to flout
The birds, pull down low limbs and taste the pricking
Of pert asperity upon his tongue,
A puckish tang too impudent for pies
But not for mockingbirds, for they have sung
Its praises often to approving skies.
So it is best to leave the loftily gleaming
Elusive small acidities to those
Who cling beside the dangling prizes, seeming
Quite sure to be dislodged if one wind blows;
But every fruiting season taste a few.
Let them explain the mocker's song to you.

Saturday

I lie on the grass and consider a daisy
Letting the drowsy hours go by.
If I really tried I could stop being lazy
But I'm just too lazy to try.

Aristocrat

The thrasher, bird of aloof and sudden ways,
Grows curiously tolerant these days
And overlooks, in view of cornbread crumbs,
Our obvious humanity. He comes
Close to the window, approving of our fare,
While we in ardent admiration stare
At his superb rich elegance of color
That makes the robin's suitable gray look duller
And the cardinal's crimson gaudy. We softly tell
Each other that he appears to know quite well
No human artist, whatever his renown,
Could reproduce the splendor of his brown.

Midsummer Invitation

The burning light that weighs our eyes,
The shadows, languid, deep,
Of leaves that sway in lullabies
Entice us all to sleep.

I really meant to stay awake
But now I've quite surrendered.
It would be rudeness not to take
A nap so warmly tendered.

Season for Independence

It's not much wonder it was in July
They signed the Declaration. Men who try
To cope with the extravagant rich growing
Of this American summer, who are hoeing
And fighting bugs and getting in the hay
Ahead of thunderstorms, might justly say,
"We've got enough to do with this big land.
It's just as well to make them understand
We can't be bothered now with minor things.
There's corn to pick. We haven't time for kings."

Farewell for a Friend

Robin, dashed against the glass
Of my window, you will pass
Through the sunlit sky no more
And never pouncingly explore
For your breakfast on my lawn,
Announce the spring or greet the dawn.

Underneath your apple tree
Seems the place for you to be
And, as least that I can do,
I plant wake-robin over you.

Commencement

It was more than wind in the hedges
Or the flurry of leaves in the sun.
It was hurry and stir and excitement
Of a new adventure begun.

Sunlight and wind in the hedges—
And young birds learning the earth,
And old birds showing them all about
Water and seeds and mirth.

Today the hedges are empty—
Say it without a sigh
For the little birds who were learning the earth
Have learned the sky.

Squirrel in the Sky

The dead elm tree is towering still
Over us and the landscape, starkly proud,
And a squirrel is capering with heedless skill
Silhouetted against a cloud.

Weightless agility high in the blue,
Traversing bare branches in frolicsome flights—
A squirrel is a rodent, that is quite true,
But a rodent with heavenly visiting rights.

Change

Summer afternoons
Nothing can possibly happen.
Leaves' heavy lassitude
Cannot be shaken.
In ponderous sunned air
No breeze can stir,
No bird shape static silence
Into song.

With an effort, we may sip ice water
And move to a shadier corner of the porch,
Causing the old dog the tremendous duty
Of flicking his tail one time against the floor.
But nothing can possibly happen.
It is summer.

Then something happens.

Leaves redden, lose weight, float, fly.
Clouds scud, scurry, scoot through the sky.
Winds whistle, whizz, whir to and fro.
Birds gather, flock, form groups, and go
And we rush to keep up with it all.
Everything happens in fall.

Unready

One golden leaf—and I, whom all
Fall's golden woods elate,
Look at my summer multitudes
Of green, beseeching, "Wait!"

I have not garnered sun enough
To need a harvest moon.
I would not part with hummingbird
And tanager this soon.

And who is weary now of roses
And tired of daisies' pearly
White greetings by abundant fields?
All goldenrod is early.

Amazing fortune plunges us
Head over heels in debt
To fall for gold, but thrifty hearts
Must always cry, "Not yet!"

Marigolds

These round exuberant ones
Appear in morning places
Like little nightcapped suns
With frills around their faces.

First of October

October dawned upon me with a glow
Of muted light from sky yet soft with rain
Shining through crimson dogwoods that bestow
Their brightness on my room through every pane
And with a boon of morning-glory blue
Blooming amazingly high above the red
Exultant leaves with raindrops shimmering through
From leaf to leaf as robins lit and fled.
A young squirrel in his first October came
And curved himself with immemorial grace
And plucked and ate a berry's rounded flame
With all of wonder in his wide-eyed face.
I would that all the world could share and see
October's dawning as it came to me.

Fall Dandelion

It could have sparked new hope, and merry,
On some drab lawn of February
Or wafted hours of childhood by
In idle pastures of July;
But how compete, belated, bold,
With goldenrod and marigold?
I smile at it and ask no reason
For joy existing out of season.

Window Watcher

The birds have been industrious all this day;
A competence of robins making merry
On dogwood boughs, with periods of play
In the birdbath, did not leave a single berry.
A diligence of sparrows gathered seeds
From withered grasses, stretching tiptoe high,
And flurried off at quite excessive speeds
When brash blue jay militia flaunted by.
A tiny greenish bird I do not know
Was everywhere and nowhere, tantalizing
Me into constant looking high and low—
A Tennessee warbler, to my best surmising.
The birds have been industrious—now the sun,
Descending, finds my own work just begun!

Perpetual Jay

The blue jay in the sassafras
Is blatant blue in gaudy gold
Flapping a shower of leaves to grass.
The blue jay in the sassafras
Flaunts out of sight, but will not pass.
So long as memory can hold
The blue jay in the sassafras
Is blatant blue in gaudy gold.

Needless Conflict

The slim Confederate mockingbird
And the Federal blue jay
Skirmished about the berries
Of the dogwood all this day.

A lightning-swift maneuver
And the blue jay was defeated.
A stubborn heavy onslaught
And the mockingbird retreated.

Forward and back they battled
Appearing strangely loath
To observe that there were brilliant
Berries enough for both.

Chinese Elm in Autumn

The Chinese elm has never quite
Learned colorful American ways,
But when the native trees are bright
With annual gold and scarlet blaze
Its leaves turn gentle golden brown
And, spinning decorously to earth,
Appear to twinkle, twirling down,
At jubilant American mirth.

Repeating Marvels

Sometimes I wonder if the Lord grows tired
Of praise expressed in my accustomed phrases
Of glorious skies and woodlands wildly fired
With passions of pure color and of hazes
That, half-concealing old, beloved hills,
Reveal new loveliness with every hour.
I would create fresh terms for joy that fills
My heart these glowing days, had I the power.
Yet since the sky is blue, predictably,
However unbelievably each year,
And oaks are red each fall, it well may be
That He, repeating marvels out of sheer
Delight in them, is pleased with gratitude
Expressed in old ways vibrantly renewed.

Pause

We saw one bright leaf falling from the tip
Of the tallest maple on the highest hill
When nothing else was stirring. Winds were still
And time paused, waiting, while it fell and fell
Past all the bright leaves, down and down and down
Until it touched dry grass and rested so.
Then time went on and as we turned to go
A hundred leaves came whirling down and down.

Here

A day of many goings
Through the bright air;
Leaf fall and wingbeat,
Slow drift and quick flare,
Startings, departings,
Everywhere, anywhere.

A day of few stayings;
Trees, sky, and I
Stably abiding
While others fly,
Going nowhere at all
Far off or near.
We arrived long ago.
We remain here.

Leavings

No owners of lawns would grieve
Nor feel the fall so fell
If summer, taking its leave,
Would take its leaves as well.

October Tulip Poplar

As gold leaves overhead
And gold leaves underfoot
Make light of loss
The bent small woman stands,
Brown as a withered leaf,
Re-storing gold; it will be winter soon.

In one veined wrinkled hand
She holds one lambent leaf,
A tulip's silhouette; profile of spring.

Garden After Frost

Not grown for ornament, asparagus
Is fragile gold, is fall's forsythia,
Is fountains of delicate yellow lightly playing
In unexpected gaiety on dull air.

Asparagus, an unctuous vegetable
With a name that can't be taken seriously—
Its useful row in the garden is transfigured
At summer's ending into a feast for the eyes.

What valued shrubbery this might seem to us
Were the spears not, edibly, asparagus.

First of November

November's tolling syllables
Bring mists to mind, and gray
Dolorous clouds. November is
A solemn word to say.

The mists are here, the clouds are here,
But one great maple tree
With clouds of golden light is still
Illuminating me;

And fragile gilt of sparrowgrass
Waves airily in dull cold.
November may depart in gray;
November came in gold.

Impostor

One leaf remaining on the branch
Is oddly like a perching bird
And often, glimpsing it by chance,
Unstirring, I have felt absurd
Annoyance that a bird should sit
And scrutinize me day by day.
A leaf has rights, no doubt, but it
Has my consent to fly away.

To All Who Cherished Summer

November's fallen leaves and widened skies
That shine through branches' candid filigrees
Are seldom deprecated by the wise
Who love essential inwardness of trees
And never have enough of heavenly space
Whether it be a festival of blue
Where celebrating clouds perform with grace
Or chastened gray with silver shimmering through.
What though the jubilee of leaves is past
And only muted grays and browns remain?
To all who cherished summer it will last
As long as they, and they accept the plain
Bestowals of November with thanksgiving,
Habitually enjoying all of living.

Force of Nature

They're bound to make snow cream
And snow forts and men
And dozens of snowballs
Again and again.

Adults may be housebound
A winter's day through
But there are things children
Are snowbound to do.

Time of Snowing

Not much of time is measured
By the hourglass of the air
With powdery lusters falling
About us everywhere.

We count most hours by shadows
Until the sun has fled
Or by our private clepsydra
Of tears unshed and shed.

But moments meted briefly
By calm descents of white
Are imprecise, unpunctual,
Immeasurable delight.

Feeder

The hulking starling lumpishly arrives
At the suet feeder, alarming chickadees
To undulating bursts of flight, and drives
His piercing needle beak at suet, to seize
And avidly devour. With every jerk
The impartial sun reveals upon his back
The royal iridescences that lurk
And glisten deep within his beggar's black.

A Place for Spring

This winter view is desolate enough—
Swatches of old snow ragged on dun grass
Where pigeons pace like pompous rocks, and bluff
Away a flock of starlings like black glass.
The sky is stony gray as pigeon backs
And from it now and then some sharp flakes fall
In a brittle avalanche that quickly slacks
To blank indifferent nothing after all.
A dismal view enough; but chickadees
Bounce through the stolid air, and cardinals blaze
A trail of hope, and we have seen these trees
Transfigured with soft blooms on April days.
Whatever hard, benumbing storms have crossed it
This view is still our own; we have not lost it.

Beak

The winter robin condescends to crumbs
Because of snow.
His bright orange beak is like a child's crayon stroke.
Its sharpness pricks us slightly; yet we know
A child would draw it so.

April Fool

Today above December earth
There floats an April sky
Whose miles of blue translucent mirth
Almost persuade the eye
That bare trees wear a leafy haze,
That lawns are greenly new,
And crocuses, before our eyes,
Are playing peekaboo.
It's skyborn fairytale and myth
But we are half-believing,
Our hearts co-operating with
This innocent deceiving.

In December

How vulnerable the small earth lies
To every wind that blows
Till heaven wraps it tenderly
In pure white swaddling clothes.

Mild Defense

"What good can be expected of a year
That starts with January?" one demanded.
"If we can live through it we're in the clear
To weather all the rest," I said with candid
Assent to her distaste for heating bills,
Post-Christmas letdown, bitter winds, and frozen
Dangerous streets, and various virus ills—
"Although it's not a month I would have chosen."
But after all a year must start somewhere
And January calls us to renewed
Resolve just when we need it most, to bear
Grim days with humor, grace, and fortitude—
And all my life I have discovered very
Good things in years that start with January!

This
Much
Space

This Much Space

Eight feet of outer space are all we need.
Eight feet of space beyond our present wall,
Enclosed, roofed, windowed, warmed will be indeed
A triumph over bounds unduly small.
Yet to achieve this sublunary aim
Earth must be deeply outraged with cement
And garden peace disrupted by our claim
Much to the birds' astonished discontent.
We must enlist extensive lengths of pine
That grew in storm, unhindered, toward the sun
To keep out wind and rain and to define
The heights to which our fond ambitions run;
But we shall live with added zest and grace
For having conquered even this much space.

Rounded

The shape of any day is circular.
The earliest clock informs us of the fact.
It may be a bubble shimmering in bright air
Or an apple resting, comfortably compact,
Within the hand, or a rugged prickly burr
Revealing gloss. But always hands must meet
And touch at the central point of every sphere
For the circle of a day to be complete.

Since We Decided

Count over now the things we have not lost:
Quiet waking in a customary room
Its polished floorboards punctually crossed
By morning's clearest radiance; the bloom
Of rosy color glorifying all
Its ordinary objects when the light
From one great maple touches them each fall—
What other room could ever be as bright?
Count gloatingly the amiable cool porch,
Most favorably remembered by all friends,
And the garden plot that noon suns never scorch
And the pine whose sturdy friendship never ends
And all the things we never loved so well
As now, since we decided not to sell.

What Women Do All Day

Wipe smudgy fingerprints from looking glasses,
Shine up the floor where someone spilled molasses,
Wash dishes, cook, sweep, dust, reply to questions,
Sew buttons on, kiss hurts, make wise suggestions,
Fall into bed when all the family's dreaming
And conscientiously refrain from screaming
At realizing all the things they got done
Are things that never show unless they're not done.

Cut and Dried

In Egypt archeologists,
Industrious with trowels,
Have rescued from oblivion's mists
Four-thousand-year-old towels
With ends cut off and then resewn
Where they had started to fray—
Soft terry towels much like our own
We're wearing out each day.

However soaked, in every age,
In the effort to make ends meet
Women don't throw in the towel with rage
But stubbornly make ends neat.

Brushoff for a Housewife

Why feel you must
With arduous care
Rearrange the dust
On table and chair?

Let this intent
Endeavor cease.
Our dust is meant
To rest in peace.

In April Winds

She hung clean clothes out in the April air,
Neatly and carefully, folding hem to hem,
And orchard winds blew fragrances of pear
And peach and apple blossoms into them.
Small meadow winds brought scent of grasses growing
And the elemental odor, fresh and rich,
Of ploughed earth; all day sunny winds were blowing
All April into every thread and stitch.
No finest-textured linen that has lain
Treasured in lavender could ever soothe
Folk to a gentler slumber than these plain
Worn cotton sheets drawn beautifully smooth.
Earth's loveliest dreams belong to those who lie
In sheets that hung in April winds to dry.

Grandmother's Postal Rate

When it was cold it didn't take
Grandmother more than half a minute
To walk down to the big mailbox
And back with all that might be in it.

But when the first warm days of spring
Began it took her half the day—
She stopped to speak to every leaf
And blade of grass along the way.

Projects

I like to see men stand around discussing
The proper way of doing anything,
Hands in their pockets, with no nervous fussing—
Paving the driveway, cutting off a wing
From the house, or adding a porch from which to
    view things,
Or putting out a hedge—with all the fun
They get from figuring just how to do things
It doesn't matter if they're never done.

Workbook for Wives

Leave a man at work alone.
Leave his work uncriticized.
Leave him strictly on his own,
Uninstructed, unadvised—
While remaining near at hand
To fetch and carry at his command.

Ex-pounded

He had a hundred things to talk about
When he was stout.
His only subject now is how to win
At getting thin.

Prescription Blank

The doctor's knowledge is unfailing
Whenever anyone is ailing.
"Avoid excitement, strain, and noise,"
He tells the mother of four small boys;
And for the trial attorney's tension,
"You must shun discord and dissension."
The mailman, worn with snow and sleet,
Is strongly urged, "Stay off your feet,"
And farmers hear with pained surprise,
"Abstain from strenuous exercise."

The doctor knows our bones and glands
And how to wield with expert hands
Sphygmomanometer and knife
But doesn't know the facts of life.

Spooky Statistics

Don't overeat, whatever you do.
Don't let yourself grow stout
For modern science proves it true
By heart attacks and gout
That the gobblin's will get you
If you don't watch out.

Conversational Pause

"I loathe clichés," he said in confidence,
At which my conscience started in dismay
And scared from mossy corners an immense,
Exhausted, sagging, spiritless array
Of terms that I had used in talk with him:
"She might have healed the breach; she might have
   broken
The vicious circle; now it's sink or swim"—
How pitiful the phrases I had spoken!
As memory, meanly faithful, shuffled all
The superannuated workers past,
The worn enfeebled figures, ready to fall,
And blank expressions left me shamed, aghast.
"That's why," my friend resumed, "I'm thankful you
Use language sparkling fresh as morning dew!"

Summing Up

I might less often be at such
A loss but that, however reckoned,
Forethought is worth just twice as much
As second.

Heightened Effect

If you let down your hair to an intimate
In vivid, vigorous phrasing
The reports that will shortly circulate
Are likely to be hair-raising.

Call Me Incomparable

"You're looking better than when we last
Met," leaves me feeling quite aghast
And wondering wildly, at each such greeting,
How frightful I looked at our last meeting—
How woefully pale, how painfully spare,
How dull of eye, how drab of hair.

To make me evermore your debtor
Please say I'm looking well, not better!

In Praise of Me

When people say, "Well, we must go,"
And stand and talk, not doing so,
I never scream, and won't, I trust,
"Indeed you must, you must, you *must!*"

Whew!

Sitting still for a moment or two
Is something children can seldom do
And after an hour of their bouncing glee
Moving's impossible for me.

Basic Requirements for Rearing the Young

Hope
And soap.

Wifely Feat

She takes good care to put the bills
Away till all is smoothly clicking
And she is sure he'll foot the bills
With little kicking.

Having Had It

While shelling out, with many a qualm,
The revenue expected,
The citizen, though far from calm,
Feels thoroughly collected.

Self-sufficient

Most people find it difficult
Sometimes, to know just what is right,
And they consider and consult
With other minds in search of light.
But not Miss Harriet; she had
One certain rule, her whole life long,
For quickly knowing good from bad,
And black from white, and right from wrong.
Whatever she didn't want to do
Was what she should. She did it, too.

Oversight

She asks no favors of her friends,
Avoids imposing on them
With scrupulous care, and fondly spends
Much time and thought upon them.

Just one kind thing she leaves undone,
Unrecognized, unheeded;
She never gives to anyone
The joy of feeling needed.

Flower Arrangement

Roses, irises, and pinks
In a green glass vase
Her neighbor brought her, with a smile
Blossoming on her face.

"I wanted you to have the best,"
She said, "because, you see,
Each flower in this bouquet has bloomed
From plants you've given me."

For One Departing

Her life was substitution;
Sparrow instead of lark,
Instead of roses, thistles,
Instead of morning, dark.

By sparrow, thistle, darkness,
Answer our request;
Let her have authentic
Heaven, after rest.

Return

He looked like someone going home,
Someone who hadn't been at home
And hadn't hoped to be at home
For many years.

We saw him run up to the house
And knock, and finally leave the house.
His face, not looking at the house,
Was harsh with tears.

Refugee

He wearies people, speaking long
In praise of stars, in praise of song.

He can't forget the dark confines
Where nothing sings and nothing shines.

The Choosers

They wander fields where summer strews
Extravagance of petals
And show, with sadly patient smiles,
Their small bouquets of nettles.

The Undeceived

April is actual only to the old,
Not to the young.

The young are rapturous over apple blossoms
And eagerly expectant of rich harvests.

The old sit quietly and are content
To see pale clouds of petals in blue air.

If harvests fail, the avid young rebel
And call the blossoms all a cruel deceit.

The old, with hungers never satisfied,
Recall the joy the fleeting blossoms gave.

New Realist

With a few bright threads from a worn-out dream
She embroiders designs of wings that gleam
And shimmer, with stitches firm and exact,
Over the stiff hard fabric of fact.

Builder

She cannot drive a nail
Nor put a shelf together
Nor even assist with castles
In child-and-seashore weather;
But her upbuilding talent
Yields endless satisfactions;
She puts the best construction
On other people's actions.

Of Blessed Memory

She can't remember names and dates,
She won't remember hurts and hates,
But she never forgets a kindness done
To her and hers by anyone.

The Shy One

She speaks her truth and hopes she is not heard.
She shows her earnest heart's intrinsic shape
In search of understanding—like a bird
With wings adjusted always for escape.

Grace by Association

Those who are fond of cats, I have observed,
Have usually a certain quiet grace
With motions pleasantly relaxed and curved
Not angular and awkward, with no trace
Of jerky hesitations such as mar
The gestures of high-tension people who
Find cats unnecessary and who are
Uninterested in the things they do.
And I have noticed often that the mind
Of one who is a cat's associate
Lacks the rigidity I'm apt to find
In people who refuse to contemplate
The swift dexterity and supple power
That any cat can teach at any hour.

Enough

"I wish I had enough to give away
To other's need," we sometimes hear one say.
If *now* he does not have enough to share
He never would, were he a millionaire.

Song for Parents

Ask of your teen-aged daughter,
Ask of your teen-aged son
No sharing of the glories
And grievings just begun;

Nor think that, having been young,
You can teach them how.
Their guarded eyes will tell you
You are not young now.

Youth's a separate country
Each explores alone.
They will share their youth with you
When their youth's outgrown.

Each Generation

They come, young, ardent, daring, in their season,
To a novel world of challenge and delight
And break their hearts for no unusual reason
And find their fiercest tragedy is trite.

The One-Talent Man

A trusting eager child, he was derided,
Made shrinkingly aware of lack of worth
When one he loved rejected work he prided
Himself on, and he hid it in the earth.

So later, entrusted with one precious thing,
He hid it lest he lose it, for he feared.
He bears his punishment; and time will bring
An equal recompense to one who jeered.

Reflections of the Bridegroom's Mother

She's taking him for better or for worse,
And I've no doubt she'll love and cherish him
Even when he breaks her wedding china
And says her new hat needs a wider brim.

But she won't know what it was like to cherish
Him when he hid a bullfrog in his trunk
And love him when he clipped the neighbor's poodle
And lost an altercation with a skunk.

New Afternoon

An old neglected field,
With a small brook half-concealed
In weeds, is something more
For children to explore.

"Oh, look, oh, look, look, look!"
Cries Debbie in a nook
Frail blue-eyed grasses gem.
I look, but not at them.

"Watch me, see how I throw
A rock, and ripples go
Around, around, around!"
I watch Brent's eyes, spellbound.

Home now, content with flowers
Soon wilting; but fresh hours—
Earth's newest afternoon—
Will not be over soon.

Letter Perfect

Miss Thompson's class today is writing letters,
Miss Thompson's class in Knoxville, Tennessee,
Reports on guppies, parakeets, and setters
To unknown Kansas City friends-to-be.

Miss Thompson's class today is proudly telling
Of homes and pets and Smoky Mountain bears
With cautious penmanship and careful spelling
And hopes of letters in reply to theirs.

Miss Thompson's David, after twice rewriting
His letter to correct one little, lonely
Mistake, is finding victory exciting—
He *didn't* write O-L-N-Y for only!

Encouragement for Teachers

Among the shoddy work, half-understood,
The nearly excellent, the almost good,
You will discover, some rewarding day,
Some work that unmistakably rates *A*.

First Song for Timothy

Timothy hay
Gives excellent yields
Of lively fragrance
In sunlit fields,
But never such whiffs
Of fresh sweet joy
As does bathed and powdered
Timothy boy!

Takeover

When Timothy visited Great-grandmother
He regarded her gravely like any other
Strange person seeking his cherished baby
Approval, poised between *yes* and *maybe*;
Then suddenly decided, beaming sweetly,
She belongs to him—and she does completely!

Height of Enjoyment

How greatly the sky expands,
How joyfully sunlight spills
When Timothy, laughing, stands
Knee-high to daffodils.

Winning

The challenge of being Timothy's brother
And of living up to Timothy
Might well have daunted any other
But Randy gurgles beguilingly.

Parents and grandparents keep on saying
Timothy's pretty and smart and sweet.
As competition he's quite dismaying
But Randy chuckles, waving his feet.

Timothy isn't competition.
Randy and Timothy understood
From the first, and beaming glad recognition
They are perfectly happy in brotherhood.

Advance

Timmy's little brother Randy
Recently became big brother
To their little sister Robin.
Only yesterday their mother
Heard him speak his first full sentence
With a warmly loving coo
As he greeted Robin gently,
"Hello, little Robbie Sue."

To Joseph at Three Months

Seeing your smile of rapturous approval,
Your happy approbation of the world,
Feeling my finger clutched beyond removal
By wee rose-petal fingers tightly curled
About it, gazing deep in joyous wonder
At the enchanted wonder in your eyes,
I think that time has made a blessed blunder—
You are your mother in a small boy's guise.
You have her smile, indeed, for she is smiling
At you the very smile she smiled at three
Months old, and you return it, gay, beguiling,
Each mirroring the other merrily.
With her love, and our love for her and you—
No wonder you smile and laugh enough for two!

Duplicated

Joseph's sister Janice
Has Joseph's sparkling eyes
And Joseph's beatific smile
Of innocent surprise,
But Joseph has not lost them
Nor has their mother, Joan;
She has three sets of each now
And they are all her own!

First Formal

She studied every hint
On fabric, hue, and styling
That she could find in print
And kept them all for filing.

Her dress, her hair, her nails,
Attended to with passion
For exquisite details
Were glamourously in fashion.

Yet she had cause to grieve
Because it wasn't stated
The heart worn on the sleeve
Is hopelessly outdated.

The Gentle One

She will be one of those to whom folk turn
Instinctively for warmth and reassurance,
For consolation, and the steadfast power
Of courage that is more than mere endurance.

And she will give them all they ask, for she
Was clearly born to play the giver's part.
Oh, may there be one wise enough to seek
The shy, soft laughter hidden in her heart,

To Keep

What I want most of all to keep
Of this October day
Is not the sky's unclouded sweep
Or the dogwood, berry gay,
In the tender light, or the one red bough
On the giant maple tree,
Though, gazing, I would make them now
A glowing part of me;
But best is seeing the glory shine
On a child too awed to stir
For a moment, with all that is deeply mine
Becoming part of her.

Birthright

I wish that I could give you, child I love,
All that I have learned from any tree,
All that winds have told me, all that stars have taught,
All that little rains have said to me.

But such a gift is needless, child I love.
Though all they ever said to me is true
Trees and wind will whisper, stars and rain will teach
Other lessons, other truths to you.

Book
Review

Book Review

She stands before us joyously relating
How thrilled she was to find the author stating
That careful tests, exhaustive and precise,
Have fully proven that giraffes and mice
Have in their necks, in some mysterious way,
Exactly the same number of vertebrae.

How shameful to admit that I must be
Devoid of intellectuality,
Of proper scientific interest
And learning's pure, enthusiastic zest
Because, however culturally willing,
I do not find this information thrilling.

The Satirists

How gloatingly they point to contradictions
Between our conduct and expressed convictions,
Compelling us to make our lives sincere—
They also serve who only stand and sneer.

Handy Rule

"The only time I can think of when it is improper
for a woman to wear gloves is when she is eating."
Emily Post

Read now the glad pronunciation,
The tidings of emancipation
From every lurking, nagging doubt
On when to wear or go without
Your gloves. You're socially correct,
Impeccable, should you elect
To wear them swimming 'mid the fishes,
Bathing a baby, washing dishes,
Manicuring your fingernails,
Typing your letters, robbing mails,
Or knifing foes. No brows will lift
And no punctilious friend be miffed
For all is proper etiquette
If, hand in glove, you haven't et.

Parenthetical Observation

I like the intimate and private look
Parentheses give words, and I expand
Importantly to them just as I do
To secrets whispered low (behind one's hand).

Grappling with a Yaffle

"Wagtails and the yaffle visit occasionally."
                    Richard Church, *Small Moments*

In a book I found a mention
Of a certain bird, a yaffle,
Put there, surely, with intention
To astound, distract, and baffle.

Is a yaffle just a trifle?
Will a yaffle's feathers ruffle?
Are its colors quite an eyeful?
Does it hop or run or shuffle?

Is a yaffle known to nature?
Ineffectually I riffle
Pages of bird nomenclature,
Judging yaffles purely piffle.

Ah, at last! A yaffle's merely
A green woodpecker, nothing harmful,
In English dialect—and, fairly—
Yaffle also means an armful.

Housing Authority

All bluebirds, this authoritative tome
Assures me, need their nesting boxes set
On posts just six feet high, to feel at home;
To please a flicker one must not forget
To place his residence on a high dead stub
Above surrounding leaves; no martins frown
Upon white homes, but other birds will snub
Bright-painted ones, preferring gray or brown.
How gently innocent an occupation
This author's is, who carefully acquires
Much intimate, exhaustive information
On robins' preferences and wrens' desires
And earnestly exerts himself to please
The tastes of cardinals and chickadees!

Typographical Error

An asterisk,
A little star,
Is used to show
Where footnotes are;
But it, in any
Apt design
Would indicate
Where high lights shine.

Song of Solomon

I Kings 4:30-33

Solomon was the wisest king that ever the world has
seen.
His knowledge startled the sages of old and van-
quished Sheba's queen.
He spoke three thousand proverbs and his songs were
a thousand and five
And he spoke of birds and beasts and fish and all
small things alive;
But the words that declare his wisdom above all
others are these
From the ancient chronicle's pages: "And Solomon
spoke of trees."

He spoke of the tiny hyssop that springs forth out
of the wall
As well as of Lebanon's cedars; King Solomon spoke
of all,
Of their glorious grace of growing, their green benefi-
cent shade
And the strength of their steadfast beauty in the
Temple of God displayed.
Oh, Solomon was the wisest king, his sayings shall
never cease,
And the fruit of his tree of knowledge was the know-
ledge and love of trees!

Upon a Definition

"The larch; a tree of graceful habit." Some
Precise, restrained, and usually circumspect
Impartial lexicographer has become
Moved by a breath of feeling to select
So gently, beautifully apt a phrase
As this to make his definition clear
Since nowhere else in all the book does praise
Resembling this, for any tree, appear.
The elm is "graceful" yes, but it is not
"Of graceful habit," always surely so.
Poplar is "slender"; as for others, what
Genus and use they are is enough to know.
So where the tidy definitions march
I sense a leaning toward the pliant larch.

Lilac

"A color of low brilliance
And medium saturation"
According to Webster's carefully
Uncolored explanation.

He errs—for all the Aprils
That keep my heart content
Are highly saturated
With lilac color and scent.

Exile from Winging Skies

(W. H. Hudson)

His heart, sad exile in a London room,
Pulsed to the wingbeat of long vanished birds.
Before the Eskimo curlews met their doom,
Before great plains were fenced for trampling herds,
He rode enormous Argentina plains,
A boy with eager wonder in his eyes,
To see huge migrant flocks and hear brief strains
Of fugitive music from the winging skies.
Through patient decades in an alien land
Of uncongenial streets he saw, instead,
The bird he watched, in his young journeyings, stand
As men have pictured angels, wings outspread,
And heard through crash of traffic, over and over,
The wild sweet calling of the upland plover.

Who May Be a Poet

The lonely, the rejected
Who love on, undeterred,
May speak the unexpected
Inevitable word.

Out of Context

(First part of *Henry IV*, act 1, scene 1)

A harmlessly poetic act, to bring
All birds that Shakespeare mentioned to our skies—
Had Hotspur not resolved to give the King
A starling, with malicious enterprise;
One taught to speak a hated name "to keep
His anger still in motion." That one bird
Caused all these restless hordes that swoop and sweep
And leave no lawn nor tree nor wrath unstirred.
Few nightingales survived to soothe our gloom.
Usurping starlings lived to overwhelm
More space than Henry won by Richard's doom
By ousting bluebirds from their rightful realm.
We cannot blame the Bard; he made it plain
That any gift of starlings is a bane.

"Philip-Sparrow"

In Shakespeare's time a sparrow's usual name
Was Philip, as a wren's is Jenny now,
And any rush of sparrows has good claim
To giving a day a fillip, I'll allow.

In freezing rain the small brown birds pursue
Weed seeds industriously, in cozy clans.
"Whatever things are honest, just, and true,"
Is still the message of Philippians.

Exception to Thoreau

When Thoreau and his brother made a camp
Near Hookset in New Hampshire, rainclouds shed
Down water till supplies were very damp—
"But still we kept our thoughts dry," Thoreau said.

It may have been dry humor. But of all
Men I would have expected him to be
Glad to expose his thinking to the fall
That nourishes the grass root, flower, and tree.

As for myself, I never would deny
My thoughts to rainclouds' excellent bestowing.
I wouldn't think of keeping my thoughts dry—
I want them wet and fresh, alive and growing.

The Different Worlds of Dickinson and Thoreau

To Emily "This remarkable earth"
By being, justifies
A quiet trust in infinite
Continuing surprise.

But Henry, though "This curious world"
Is good for pondering,
Will not, in any future, be
Surprised at anything.

Southern View

New England's poets observed and spoke with spare
Authority in the dry New England way.
E. Dickinson saw yellow as most rare
And Frost averred that nothing gold can stay.
No yellow jasmine blooms in February?
No dandelions, forsythia, daffodils?
No lemon lilies making summer merry?
No goldenrod upon October hills?
Yellow chrysanthemums, long-lasting, bold,
And marigolds have kept my view alight
Until sweet shrub and mock orange leaves turned
    gold.
Yellow may be a rare and fleeting sight
To anyone who "sees New Englandly"
But it is plenteous in Tennessee.

Scope

The modern critic favors the specific;
No poet should mention birds unless he knows
And states in terms acutely scientific
If they are thrushes, robins, jays or crows.

"A single bird" in Emily's dominion
Propounds a song without defining words,
And we choose which should be, in our opinion,
Denominated "Presbyterian birds."

Americans in Europe

"From London we went by little rivers in a land
just big enough."
Thomas Wolfe, *Look Homeward, Angel*

The old lands fit the people.
They are a proper size
With no excessive spaces
And no immoderate skies.

The old lands are just big enough—
No wildly empty air
Nor overwhelming distances;
But some who travel there

Feel fierce and lonely hunger
For the sprawling land they know,
A land that fits no human,
A land in which to grow.

Creativity

It knows no appeasing,
It knows no greed.
Its seed is hunger,
Its soil is need.

You will sow and tend
And at last there will rise
A harvest that almost
Satisfies.

The White House Trees

John Quincy Adams had New England's elm
Implanted deeply in the White House grounds
And it is standing now, a mighty realm
Of leaves that rustle with New England sounds.
Though Andrew Jackson had no use for tact,
Nor Adams either, his magnolia tree
Is far enough away not to detract
From the elm with petals breathing Tennessee.
If Benjamin Harrison seems colorless
To history, his scarlet oaks recall
His love of color; huge Cleveland could express
A taste for Japanese maples, dainty, small.
The trees that presidents select disclose
Their hearts; would there were one that Lincoln
　　chose!

Lincoln

The praises men have given him can never
Be adequate to his immensity.
Who can describe the Rockies? Who can ever
Find words to fit the towering redwood tree?
Say of him only, when you speak his name,
That he was worthy of them; say that he
Alone of all Americans became
As great as all Americans should be.

In the Library

April 5, 1968

The news has spread.
The clergyman, Nobel Peace Prize winner,
Who dreamed that the American dream is for all
   Americans,
Is dead,
Shot in his dreaming head
Almost as if he were a president.

In the library,
Surrounded by the works of Jefferson, Lincoln,
   Thoreau, Whitman, Sandburg,
Students tell the gentle darkskinned assistant,
"I'm glad that fellow's dead,"
And grin at seeing her wince
At their mannerly endorsement of murder.

The same students see, on the television screen,
Rioting, looting, black
Smoke rising around the white
Dome of the Capitol
And, outraged, cry, "Why
Do they want to act like that?"

Incredibly, hopelessly
They really wonder.

Atlantis

On the lost fabled island of our dreaming
All people were courteous and life was seemly
With wise simplicities of truth and justice
In air that always glowed with kindly luster.

Always on all known islands of our waking
People hurt one another with mistaken
Kindness and half-truths heavily asserted,
And sun and wind are perilous and uncertain.

Why do we dream that any island ever
Was otherwise? We innocently revel
In legend, searching our ordinary sea
For the island that might have been and still may be.

Correction to Dylan Thomas

"Do not go gentle"—little matter how,
Tempestuous or tame, if there is no
Return; nor do we say, "Do not go now,"
But simply, passionately, "Do not go."

The Warrior

The glorious Hector, going to his doom
In battle, knowing that his faithful wife
Might meet the prisoner's fate of shame and gloom,
Bearing among his foes a servile life,
And that his son, who shrank from him in dread
As from a brilliantly ferocious stranger
Because of the bronze helmet on his head,
Might be left helpless in red blazing danger—
Great Hector, with his glory undefiled,
Took time to say good-bye, took time to bow
In prayer for weeping wife and trembling child:
"Let this my son become as I am now!"
And Homer does not mention anywhere
If Hector's son was soothed by Hector's prayer.

On Prayer Poems

Most poets at times express
In verse their supplication,
Their gratitude and grief
And awe and adoration.

I trust no editor
Within the heavenly mansion
Rejects an earnest prayer
For faulty rhyme or scansion.

Until the Word

Not till the Word
Was said by God
Did light exist
Or sky or sod.

Not till the one
Describing word
Is said by man
Does any bird,

Or any leaf
Or any dim
Star perfectly
Exist for him.

Words

I am sustained
In soul and mind
By great words, spoken
To all mankind.

But the best words
My heart has known
Were small words, spoken
To me alone.

Of
Light
and
Shade

Of Light and Shade

"Forget all sorrow," people say, who are
Considered wise. "Forget each sad event
That you have known, lest the remembrance mar
Today's tranquillity and glad content.
Remember only good." But who has ever
Found perfect good untouched by any flaw,
And when was grief so absolute it never
Held hope of deepening faith and strengthening awe?
If I forget all sorrow then I must
Forget friends' understanding, dear concern
And all the sympathy and patient trust
That only sorrow helped my heart to learn.
So mixed are light and shade that if I could
Forget all grief I must forget all good.

Wisdom

Those who have suffered and grown strong
May have a right to say
To those who suffer, "There is strength
And wisdom from dismay."

Those who have suffered and grown strong
Are silent, having learned
Man's wisdom, like his suffering,
Is separately discerned.

We Shall Recall

I hope there may be laughter where he is
Since it was by his laughter we were saved
From many griefs, and it is by the power
Of his remembered laughter we have braved
The terror of his absence, and have found
Within our own hearts something of the strong
Courageousness and faith from which his laughter
Rose like a lifting challenge and a song.
Perhaps he has no need of laughter now,
Having all joy. But through the lonely years
We shall recall his laughter and shall pray
That we may find him when our vision clears
Laughing at all the little jokes we loved
Without the earthly undertone of tears.

Unconquered

The blow that might have felled her once
Descends unnoticed now
Since she received the mightiest stroke
Of all and did not bow.

She lives in stanch unwavering
Uprightness nothing can deform,
Forever greater than any tempest,
Stronger than any storm.

Home Place

"You say you went back there? How did it look?
They've planted peach trees, as we wanted to,
Outside the kitchen windows, dammed the brook,
And screened the porch? I wonder how they knew
To do all that! We talked about it so
And planned just how to fix things when we could
I guess they almost couldn't help but know
From living in the house. Well, well, that's good.
It's nice to know they've realized all our wishes.
I know that woman does her housework well
Looking at peach blooms while she dries the dishes.
I only hope they never have to sell.
Go look at it myself? Well, no. Somehow
I couldn't say good-bye again—not now."

Invincible

"Three doctors said I would die young,"
My mother remarked at eighty-two,
And I replied, "You'll never be old
At any age. Their words were true."

Of Loving Little Objects

We who love little objects, rendered dear
By long association, have this much
That we can keep with us through the severe
Sharp hurt of leaving our own place. The touch
Of a little Dutch girl pitcher that has held
Tulips of many springs and the smile upon
A tiny china gentleman's face, that quelled
Quick tears, remain when larger things are gone.
If we must leave the sunny generous rooms,
The window with its wide familiar view,
And the garden's sweet processional of blooms
And go where all is cramped and strangely new,
No change, at least, is great enough to sweep
Away small treasures—small enough to keep.

A Different Joy

Who lives with sadness values best
Happiness seen and unpossessed;
Absolute joy in children's faces,
The curve of bliss a puppy traces,
Birds flying high, fish swimming deep
That do not mourn and need not weep.
Whose hours and days and years are sad
May give warm praise when some are glad.

Remembered Evenings

We sold the farmhouse many years ago
But spring returns whoever owns the land
And hearts return to where they were at home
When blooms emerge and little leaves expand.

There were benignant evenings in the spring
When we would rest, she very old, and I
Never so young as I was thought to be,
And look through blossoms at the glowing sky.

I wonder if any sit beside our window
And look out through the petaled cherry tree
And rock and breathe a little thankful prayer.
I ask that this may be.

Alternative

"Better to light a candle
Than to curse the dark"—
But if one can kindle
No enlivening spark
And has no smallest taper
For flame to feed upon—
One may bless the dark
And rest in it, till dawn.

City Time

"All seasons move too slowly in the city,"
He said with vehemence. "A city spring
Comes poking in and almost rouses pity
Shying at frosts, scared stiff of everything.
A country spring comes rollicking and throwing
Flowers at you all at once until you're dizzy,
Heedless of frost or snow or icy blowing
Because it's got a job to do—it's busy.
Same way with other seasons. All the trees
Start turning here in August and aren't good red
Till mid-November, and winters brawl and freeze
Clear into May. The plain truth is," he said,
Stating a theory entirely his,
"City time is the slowest time there is."

Reluctant Materialists

For shriveled dreams and aching days—
A cup of tea, a hearthfire's blaze.
The young are shocked that any find
Relief in these for the wrenched mind;
But they will come as well as we
To warming fire and soothing tea,
Needing the homely help they give
To alien griefs all must outlive.

Title

I like the way each country man I know
Speaks of his home. He calls it just "the place"
As if there were no other. The quiet slow
Assurance in his voice and in his face
Suggests no need of self-assertive "my"
Prefixed to "place." Ask why and he would stare.
The place, of course, I think he would reply
Is his or he would not be living there.
And it is never "the house," "the home." The sound
Is far more generous so you understand
The place includes some ampleness of ground,
The place is where a person can expand.
How enviable this deep content of his
In having a place and knowing where it is.

Childhood Hill

On my hill, hot and lone,
I half remembered things half-known.
Meanings shared with field and wood
I very nearly understood.
Mysteries of earth and sky
I would fathom by and by.
I barely missed remembering then
And have not come so near again.

Year of Sweet Peas

One of the years the family mentions most
We call the year the sweet peas blossomed well.
Along the fence you couldn't see a post
For flowers like butterflies charmed by a spell
Resting a moment before taking flight,
The largest blossoms and the deepest hues
I've ever seen. It was a pure delight
To gather bouquets sweet with morning dews
For kin and friends. A dozen things went wrong
For us that year; Dad's illness and Joan's fall
Kept them in bed for months, Ruth wasn't strong,
Shep died, the barn caught fire—but after all
We speak of it these days with pleasant ease
As the year we had the loveliest sweet peas.

To Fathom Joy

Often the heart must have a rest from feeling
Too much of gladness or of grief. The heart
Must wait a little while, remote, apart
From all emotion for the clear revealing
Of what emotion means; it must abstain
From pain and joy, to fathom joy and pain.

Appreciation

My childhood's silver bracelet
Wore an enchanted sheen,
And silver shining waters
All mirrored me as queen.

My spirits dance with silver
Of milkweed on the wing,
And on my finger shimmers
A pearl and silver ring.

Always allured by silver
For pleasure and for wear
Why should I be regretful
At silver in my hair?

Ornate

This compliment, sincerely offered, seems
As inappropriate to my work as though
One pinned a dazzling burst of rhinestone gleams
Upon a simple dress of calico.

In jeweled words appealing lusters lie.
Gem-studded phrases make a fine display.
Almost regretfully I put it by
For the little sterling pin I wear each day.

New Highway

Heat is cemented close beside
The house. The curtains all are drawn
And windows closed, that opened wide,
And air-conditioners moan on
And on in daily elegy
For breathing earth and shaded grass
As, where cool pastures used to be,
The fuming automobiles pass.

Folk stay inside; they do not care
To risk encountering the concrete
Implacable enmity of glare
And hard hostility of heat
Where once, beneath a tolerant sky,
They worked in friendly shade all day
With clover breezes blowing by
And sighed that summer could not stay.

—

To Engineers

Leave little roads
Where bullfrogs doze
By trifling creeks
Bulldozers cannot find.

Leave deep soft marshes
Where cattails swish
And small trails go
Where trailers never come.

Leave, please,
Roads that go nowhere;
Else, on superhighways,
All may be lost.

Intimations

The good for which we search
Is never wholly known.
A glimpse, a hint, a touch—
And we go on alone.
Yet the hint, fleeting, gone,
Assists our keeping on.

Prescription for Pride

Carry defeat
With a conquering air
Lest passers pity,
Lest strangers stare.

Shelter sorrow
In shimmering pride
Lest friend deplore,
Lest foe deride.

But weep, weep well
When you're all alone
Lest your heart congeal
To a cold small stone.

Forfended

There is no certain shelter
Against uncertainty
That can withstand disaster
Impregnably;

Except as spirits armored
With fortitude have won
Security from knowing
There is none.

Hopeful of Being

Hers was a trite life—
ABC's and the other children making fun of her
    clothes.
She knew the ABC's were old but not that tears
Had splashed in dust as a child ran home alone
Ever before.

It was all quite ordinary—
The shame of not dating and the stiff silence of the
    one date she had,
The typing job and the apartment she tried to brighten
With condensed books and paint-by-number pictures;
She learned that tears were never unusual.

She died, crippled by arthritis, in a retirement home,
Saying, "Father, into Thy hands"—
Timidly hopeful of being, out of all the millions of
    trite people,
Considered unique by One.

Though It Be Little

It is not needful that we feign conviction
Or shape our thoughts to some unquestioned creed
But that we use whatever faith we have
Though it be little as a mustard seed.
Until we put our faith into our actions
We cannot know how much our faith is worth,
As mustard seed can never grow and flourish
Until it is committed to the earth.

Never by Wishing

Friendship
Occurs when two people
Momentarily,
Simultaneously
Escape the disguises of appearance, formality, cus-
tom
The witch's curse inflicted on them at birth.

Friendship
Is when people
Come true.

Keepsakes

I shall not put your little gifts away,
The perky chickadee you whittled for me,
The bowl with sunset colors burned in clay,
The book we read together when skies were stormy.

Once I could hardly bear the least reminder
Of vanished radiance, of friendship past.
Now I am somewhat wiser, somewhat kinder,
Not blaming rainbows that they do not last.

Apart

If ever it might have been
That ever you and I
Breathed lilac air together
Beneath an April sky,
Or ever heard together
In woodsy twilight hush
The little lilting praises
Of a hidden thrush,
Or climbed old hills together
When trees released stored light
In golden showers, or slowly,
Bright. . .bright. . .bright. . .
If ever it might have been
I should have been glad.
That you wish it might have been
Makes my heart less sad.

Poise

I must move softly now,
My face composed and still.
My heart is a flagon filled to the brim with tears.
I must move carefully lest any spill.

To a Favorite Correspondent

The guest who interrupted when you wrote
The letter I received today—the guest
To whom you are immediate, not remote,
In space—received, no doubt, your welcoming best
Of homemade cookies and good conversation.
She was most fortunate who had your smiles
As well as words of gentle commendation
That come to me across unhindering miles.
But I do not begrudge your guest her share
Of your attention and encouragement.
I know that you, perceptively aware,
Make each one individually content
Because your letter made this morning shine
For me with words that are entirely mine.

Frozen

The strange day he left us
He walked in new snow.
We stared through dim twilight
Watching him go.

That night the snow froze
And day after day
We must see his footprints
Going away.

Shirley

She cherishes, as women do, her own,
And yet with a child's deep wondering respect
For bloom on butterflies, for silver blown
From dandelions; she would no more expect
To make her husband, child, or friends conform
To any design of hers than she would try
To dictate color to a crocus corm
Or teach a hummingbird which way to fly.
She seeks, with gentle ardor, friends who share
Her treasuring sense of life and gives them each
Complete acceptance, unremitting care
In the lonely places love can seldom reach,
And the greatest gift the loving can confer;
The boon of being totally safe with her.

Of Work Approved

"Thank you," the letter said,
"Because you have not wasted
The talent given you."
I, knowing how I tasted
Failure and doubt and fear,
Seeing many a shrug and nod
As I worked on, say only
"Thank God, thank God, thank God."

To Eva

Now as I name the blessings of a year
Most mercifully blessed in many ways,
A year in which harsh undertones of fear
Changed into gentle symphonies of praise,
A year of work rewarded far beyond
Expectancy, a year of dreams come true—
I count as richest gift of all the bond
Of comradeship uniting me to you.
Because the grief and laughter we have shared,
The sympathy by which our love has grown,
Have given me greater joy than I had dared
Believe could possibly become my own,
All this Thanksgiving Day my heart shall spend
In offering earnest thanks for you, my friend.

Love's Ways

We temper our tone
To another's hearing,
Relinquish a joy
For another's cheering,
Slacken our pace
When another's is slowing—
Love is the hindrance
That keeps us going.

Pause for Consideration

I frequently neglect due tabulation
Of the essential mercies of my days.
Though I would feel dismay and indignation
Were they withdrawn, I fail to offer praise
For healthful food prepared with loving care
(And yet how many moan for daily bread),
For shelter, work to do, and clothes to wear
And sight of a fluff of new moon overhead.
To be among the ones who take for granted
The bare necessities that others lack,
Whose praise is stirred by a wedge of wild geese
    slanted
Against the sky, by a feathery snow-etched track,
Or a round small face beatified by jam—
Oh, may I know how fortunate I am!

Unacknowledged, Unpossessed

A thank-you negligently tossed
To Heaven for special favors
By one whose lips are seldom crossed
By prayer's authentic savors
Is, doubtless, courteously received
By charitable Heaven
Grateful when one has not bereaved
Himself of all good given.

Unless We Guard Them Well

Perhaps the children of a future day
Between picnics on Venus and the moon
And explorations of the Milky Way
Will come and spend a summer afternoon
Among the quaint old-fashioned people, asking,
"And did you really see a robin, sir?
And even a clover field with cattle basking?
And could you tell us just what daisies were?"
Let us speak carefully of the long ago
Lost days when earth was green, and country air
Was filled with winging song and petaled glow
Lest any yearning listener may declare,
"Oh, I would give the moon if I had heard
A thrush, or ever seen a hummingbird!"

Index

Index

123

124